Nibbles

June Crebbin

Illustrated by Susan Hellard

CAMBRIDGE
UNIVERSITY PRESS

Max liked riding. He liked riding Nibbles,
but he had to be careful . . .

because Nibbles liked nibbling.

One Saturday morning, Mum and James took Max to the stables.

"Have a good ride," said Mum. "Give our love to Nibbles."

"I will," said Max. He waved goodbye.
James waved his teddy.

Max went to find Nibbles.

"Hello, Nibbles," he said, patting her neck.
Nibbles nibbled Max's ear.

"Ouch!" said Max.

Max helped to put the saddle on. He kept
a careful eye on Nibbles.

When everyone was ready, they set off.
Max was behind a boy on a grey pony.

"Don't let Nibbles get too close," said
the boy.

"I won't," said Max. "I know what she's
like."

The ponies trotted down the road. At the
bend in the road, they turned onto a track.
Suddenly, Nibbles put her head down.

Max nearly fell off.

"Hey!" he shouted.

Nibbles nibbled some grass.

"Oh no you don't," said Max, pulling her head up. "You don't need grass now."

The track went across a field and then
into a wood. Some of the trees had very low
branches. Max had to put his head down
to miss them.

But Nibbles put her head up. She bumped
Max on the nose.

"Ouch!" said Max.

Nibbles nibbled some leaves.

"Oh no you don't," said Max. "You don't
need leaves now."

They came out of the wood into another field. Over the field they rode like the wind. Nibbles loved to go fast. When they came to a gateway, Nibbles went *too* fast.

She bumped into the grey pony in front.
Then she nibbled the pony's tail. But the
pony didn't like it. He shot through the
gateway!

"Hey!" shouted the boy.

"Sorry," said Max.

Max tried hard to stop Nibbles from
nibbling anything else. But as they reached
the path leading up to the stables, Nibbles
put her head down again into the long grass.

"Ugh!" said the boy in front. "She's nibbling something brown and furry."

Max pulled Nibbles' head up. He saw something in the long grass.

"Well," said Max, "you don't need that, whatever it is."

At the stables, Mum was waiting with James. James was crying. He was crying so hard that he couldn't lick his ice-cream. Nibbles turned her head. She tried to nibble the ice-cream.

James screamed. He snatched his hand
away. The ice-cream fell onto the ground.
Nibbles moved – and trod on it!

"Sorry," said Max.

"I'll get him another one," said Mum. She
took James into the farm shop.

Max jumped off Nibbles and helped to take off her saddle.

When Mum and James came back, James was holding another ice-cream but he was still crying.

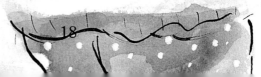

"Why is he still crying?" said Max.

"He's lost his teddy," said Mum. "I know he had it when we left the car."

Suddenly, Max thought of something –
something lying in the long grass.

"Just a minute," he said. "I think I know
where it is!"

He ran down the path to the gate.
He looked in the long grass.

There was the teddy. Max picked it up.
It was a bit soggy. He ran back to James.

"Here's your teddy!" said Max.

James hugged his teddy. He licked his
ice-cream and grinned.

"Thank you, Max," said Mum. "That was
clever."

"It was Nibbles!" said Max. "*She* found it!"

"Well," said Mum. "You're *both* clever!"

She went into the shop and came back with two ice-creams.

"Here you are," she said. "One for you . . .

. . . and one for Nibbles!"